Myth-Busti
Payme॒ ⸻ॡॡ७Ⴝtry

COPYRIGHT © Bart Kohler, CPP
January 2018

Printed in the United States of America

Bart Kohler, CPP
3286 Highland Park
North Canton OH 44720
yourcpp@gmail.com
855-255-7291

Special thanks to:
Carla Rado
Casie Mruk
Jada Weiler
Christine Vick
John Heiermann

Table of Contents

1.0 Legal Disclaimer

This material and information are for educational purposes only. No representation is made regarding their accuracy, completeness, or timeliness. This material, information, author or presenter makes no guarantees or promises. The material or information made available is not intended to and does not constitute any type of professional or legal advice. Accordingly, you should not act or rely on any information provided herein as legal advice for any purpose and should always seek the professional or legal advice of a competent counsel in your jurisdiction as it pertains to you specifically and not the generalized information provided in this material.

The author shall have no liability with respect to the information provided. Under no circumstances and under no theory of any applicable law or regulation shall the author be liable to anyone for any damages of any kind of arising tort, contract, strict liability or otherwise from access or use of or inability to access or use this material or information from any action taken or not taken by the author.

The opinions are not in any way an endorsement or representation of any association or associations, but solely those of the author.

1.1 You, I wrote this book for YOU!

Everyday I meet merchants just like you. Smart, hard working, and talented people who want to run their business and provide a service to the public while making an honest profit. Unfortunately, if you want to accept electronic payments you are forced to play a game, except no one gave you a rule book. This information will serve as that rule book for you. We will dispel the myths and begin to explain more in depth the functions of the payments industry. The electronic payments and the technology that you choose to use to conduct those payments becomes your cash flow. The number one reason that businesses go under is lack of capital. Cash flow is the lifeblood of your business.

Thank you for taking the time to invest in your business and in understanding the electronic payments industry from the very important and critical aspect of your cash flow. Cash flow is the lifeblood of your business, so it's important that you ask yourself a few questions: What do I really know about electronic payments? Who did I learn this information from? Where and who did they learn it from?

Processing companies process payments. Most banks do not process payments, in most cases their staff knows very little about the electronic payments industry. In fact, they only know what they have been told to tell you. The bottom line is you are on your own, and you really have very few trusted expert resources on your side. This book is your resource. Let's face the truth, you will be accepting electronic payments at your business for years or even decades. Take an hour and read through this book. After all, I wrote it just for YOU.

2.0 Evolution Of Payments

Payment is defined as, "Something that is given to someone in exchange for something else." Money, services, properties, rewards or incentives can all be used as payments. Originally, people would use the barter system, trading one thing for another thing, and thus commerce had begun. Fast forward to today where we generally have one form of acceptable payment, money, but now even money has taken different forms. Money can be cash or coins, checks, credit or debit cards, cell phones, rings and wearables, and now in many respects money has become virtual; just digitized currency. The expansion into virtual money allows payments and financial technology companies and their competitors to change their shape and function even further as we move into a dynamic, ever-changing and ubiquitous system. Loyalty and reward programs, characterized by skymiles and cash back programs, have become a strong motivator in the spending behaviors of customers by offering incentives for those customers to spend money while also dictating where to spend it. I will provide more details on this later on.

If we look at payments today we see that 70 percent (70%) of all consumer goods and purchases are paid for electronically. As these payment methods change it is important for business owners to adjust with the payments industry to ensure they will continue to get paid quickly and securely. In fact, some sources say that merchant services are likely one of the top five highest expenses that your business incurs. Knowing this fact as a business owner, you may want to ask: How does a merchant get paid? What takes place when an electronic payment is made?

When payment is presented by a customer for goods or services, there is first a bill, invoice or tabulation of goods. This can be calculated by hand or can be rung up as part of a point of sale (POS) or inventory management system (IMS). Products or services can even be purchased online to be shipped or picked up at a store. These are called omni channel purchases. There are dozens of methods of payments for consumers to choose from and hundreds of companies to choose from, as well. There is hardware, software and middleware, and so many ways for all of them to interact. Once the bill or invoice is calculated it is presented to the customer, and 70 percent (70%) of the time the customer elects to use electronic currency. The most common method? The card.

Now, I say that cards are just one form of payment, but cards can have many different purposes depending on the issuer. Actually, there are 13,000 banks and financial institutions issuing branded payment cards in the United States and these cards all seem to have their own nuances.

Some are debit or check cards that connect to your physical checking account. Others may be reward cards which pay the customer money back as an incentive to use the card, and a third category we will discuss are corporate or business cards - cards that are tied to a business account. These cards all look and act very much alike, but they are actually very different. How, you ask? Before I answer that question, let me give you a little background on payment cards.

Originally there were charge cards or credit cards. These are cards that banks issued to customers that allowed them to instantly borrow money and pay the money back in revolving installments. Interest was attached to the borrowed amount and it was basically a loan that had a plastic payment method. The bank or financial institutions issuing those cards earned interest on those loans which is how they made money. But how does it work for the business owner? How does the money get from the customer's account to the business owner's account? Who reconciles all of these trillions of transactions? What are the expenses and costs involved? Currently in the U.S. we have 850 million payment cards, 12 million POS devices processing payments for roughly 8 million businesses. This does not include the 12.1 billion devices online that can potentially make purchases from almost anywhere in the world; some are predicting that number to be 30 billion by 2020. How on earth is all of this managed?

2.1 Two Sides of Each Payment: Interchange Reimbursement

There are two basic sides to a sales transaction, a buyer and a seller, or the buyer's bank and the seller's bank.

How does the money get from point A, the buyer's bank account, to point B, the seller's bank account? The easiest way for me to explain is to draw you a word picture. Many years ago, banks wanted to give their customers a convenient way of traveling with money without the risk of losing it. Imagine if you had to carry all your cash with you everywhere you went. That's not a good practice for many reasons. Somewhere a bank decided they would give a card with an account number for customers to use at stores, where businesses also had an account at the same bank. The card or number would be presented at the point of sale, the goods would be signed for on a tab and the tabs would be added up and turned into the bank. Someone would read the tab, deduct the amount from the account holder's number and pay the merchant's account according to their account number. Pretty simple right? Until one day, a person wanted to use their payment card at a merchant's business who did not share the same bank. In order to get the money from one bank to another bank an interchange system had to be created. This is the premise of the interchange reimbursement program that we use today.

2.2 Interchange Rates, Dues, Assessments, and Fees

Interchange reimbursement fees are the rates or fees that are paid to the credit card issuing bank. That is the bank whose name is on that customer's card. Why should anyone pay? Counting the tabs for the sales became a very time consuming and a costly task for the banks. The card brands were formed as non-profit organizations to help control the issues that would arise from this fast growing system. To attract more consumers, card brand associations gave assurances to consumers designed to protect them when they made purchases at places accepting their brand of cards. The brand associations could also place rules on the processes and procedures to oversee any conflicts that needed reconciliation as payments evolved, and they still continue to do so today.

Back to the paper slips or tabs as we call them here: A merchant would go to the bank at the end of the day and deposit the cash from the day's sales along with checks and payment tabs. The tabs had to be physically counted, deducted from one account and paid into another account. However, what if that customer's account was at another bank? The merchant's bank would have to send the tab to the other bank to be calculated by another person until finally the funds were deducted and deposited into the proper account. This is a huge expense for the banks when you think of all the human labor that went into calculating, deducting and settling all these accounts. When I first entered the business it was not uncommon to find merchants processing with paper slips or tabs. The cost was around (7-10%) of the amount of the sale, so the term discount rate or discount fee was invented.

A discount rate is the amount that is discounted or deducted from the original sale. This fee amount is to pay for the cost of the service of allowing the business owner to take a card as payment and to guarantee the satisfaction of the customer based on the risk and size of the sale. If a merchant sold a product for $100.00, they would be discounted seven percent (7%) and $93.00 would be deposited into their account. The business owner would deduct the seven percent (7%) as a business expense. Card acceptance increased in popularity and the industry decided to automate part of the process; thus the credit card machine was born. It is simply a small computer modem that could call and report the account number and the purchase amount to another computer. It completes the process by obtaining an authorization and settling the amount to the proper account. There are actually far too many transactions taking place for the interchange to be instantaneous, so the bank that accepts the payment on behalf of the merchant and the acquiring bank must wait for a data dump once a month. This settles all the transactions and allows the merchants to see what it cost them to run the previous month's electronic payments.

I know I am giving you a lot of information here. In summation, there is a customer and a merchant. There is an issuing bank (the customer's bank), and an acquiring bank (the merchant's bank). The customer's bank gets paid by the merchant's bank to run the transaction. This process used to take place manually through one institution because the customer and the merchant used the same bank. Now, the card holder's bank also guarantees the sale or service. For example, let's say you buy a chair, and one month from the date of purchase, that chair starts to fall apart. Normally you contact the furniture store and exchange it or get your money back. Great... if it works out that easily. What if the store closed its doors or had a fire and no one was there to exchange or return the item or to issue you a refund? The customer needs to contact their bank (the issuing bank) and begin a dispute or retrieval request, which can result in a chargeback. A chargeback is when a merchant has been found at fault in the dispute and money is removed from the merchant's account and applied to the buyer's account in the form of a refund. Card associations monitor chargeback percentages. Merchants, with more than one percent (1%) of their sales being disputed, are put into a risk category and forced to reduce chargebacks or suffer the loss of processing privileges. Fees were needed to facilitate the transactions and discount rates to assess the risk of the transactions.

Figure 1 on the next page shows The Evolution of Payments. This figure demonstrates the relationships involved when settling an electronic payment:

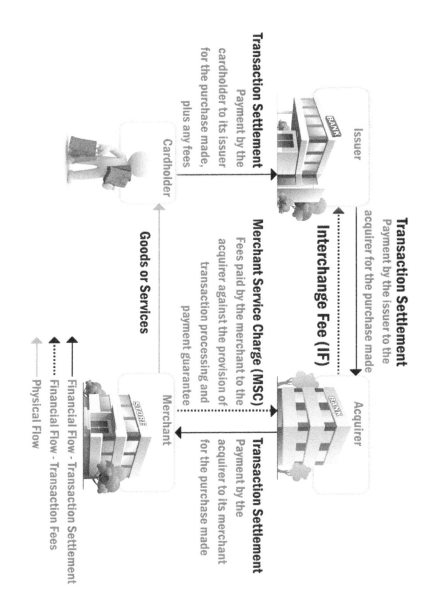

I can go further and discuss other players, which are the Independent Sales Organizations (ISO) and their agents or partners. ISOs are basically franchised agencies for the card brands and member banks. These are also the marketing arm and feet on the street that seem to be constantly soliciting merchants, but we will give you the tools to render them transparent and you will know more than many of them. We won't waste any more time than to mention that they exist and are usually your first line of service in most cases.

2.3 Risk~The Pizza and The Diet Pill

Scenario 1: When you take your family to a restaurant for pizza, you place the order, then the pizza comes out, and you eat the pizza. It is delicious! You and your family are ALL satisfied. The merchant presents a bill or check and you present the payment method. Currently, 70 percent (70%) of customers or more in that situation will use a payment card. The card is authorized and you sign the payment agreement.

Scenario 2: We have all seen the TV commercial for a product that promises to shed pounds of body fat "in just weeks." The customer orders the wonder pill, takes it as directed and gains 10 pounds. The customer can call the 800 number on the bottle, and they may offer to refund the money. Many times that is the case, but there are other instances where the company does not respond to the call or simply isn't there. That is a case where the customer, according to card association rules that protect them, asks for a dispute to be filed on their behalf. Their bank then looks at the merchant's account number that sold the goods and contacts their acquiring bank to inform them that a card holding member from the issuing bank would like to dispute a purchase made at their merchant's location or web address. The merchant usually has 10 days to reply or loses the chargeback and is fined a nominal fee by their merchant processor or acquiring bank. If a merchant has too many chargebacks a merchant may lose their right to accept payments and further action can be taken by both the card associations and law enforcement if criminal activity was involved or if laws were indeed broken. The nightmare stories are a book in themselves and for another time. Given the two examples above: Scenario 1, pizza, and scenario 2, diet pills, it is easy to see that one has a very low risk of dissatisfaction or dispute and one has a much higher risk of dissatisfaction or disputes. These are examples to show you why interchange reimbursement fees or discount rates are different for each industry. Other factors that can affect the cost of a transaction are the amount of the sale, the way in which it is being authorized, (phone, mail, web, or face to face), and the number of days until delivery; all of which can affect the cost of a transaction.

2.4 Reward, Cash Back, and Skymile Cards

Many people love to use their reward cards; myself included, as I rarely pay for airline tickets. The cards that I use pay me an incentive to use them. The money or reward that the customer receives comes from the cost of the transaction that is charged to the merchant through the interchange reimbursement fees. The merchant pays the fee to the acquiring bank who then pays the issuing bank. Finally, the promised reward is paid to the cardholder IF (s)he redeems them. When merchants complain about the cost of a transaction, we need to be reminded that the customer is getting a good portion of the discount that is being taken off of the merchant's sale. You might be asking yourself, how many different interchange categories are there? The answer is: Hundreds. New categories are created as business models and technologies develop, as risk levels change, and as regulation or law dictates. It is a dynamic industry. To recap: Risk, average ticket size, merchant type, card type, authorization method, and industry all are factors that affect the cost of a transaction. Furthermore, it is practically impossible to know the total cost of the transaction to the merchant before, during, or even shortly after a sale. In fact, merchants will not know until their statements are issued at the beginning of the month following processing. For example, August's sales statement arrives in September, just like your credit card bills do.

3.0 Two Major Elements Of A Transaction

Interchange or discount rate and transaction fee are the two major cost elements of an electronic transaction.

So far, we have discussed interchange reimbursement fees or discount rates as they are also called, but now we will introduce another key element in every sale or transaction: The transaction fee, also called the per item fee or watts fee. Back before we transmitted the payments electronically, there was only the discount rate without a transaction fee or additional fee because phone call was not being made via a terminal. However, when point of sale terminals went into use in the late 1970's and early 1980's the phone companies charged businesses for every call and a premium for long distance calls. Additionally, the banks, which are also businesses, had to pay a fee per call, so now, many pricing models have a transaction fee or communication cost. We will call it a transaction fee here to avoid using all the synonymous terms mentioned above. This is where we lose many people, so stay with me. We are going to go over some basic math principles. TEN CENTS or ($0.10) is one percent (1%) of ten dollars ($10.00). Still with me? That means if you are selling a product for ten dollars ($10.00) and your bank is charging you ten cents ($0.10), then you are paying one percent (1%) of your product sale as a transaction fee. If that sale goes down to five dollars ($5.00), then the ten cent ($0.10) fee now has double the impact and is now two percent (2%) cost of the sale. For this reason, many merchants discourage customers from making small purchases electronically because of the transaction fee cost that they must pay and the high cost associated with it when small purchases are made. Some companies have bundled rates, but the truth is that those models are quickly disappearing or have other hidden fees. One very popular product that we will not mention by name advertises a flat rate on swiped transactions only, but the company loses millions and is now raising rates and adding transaction fees on low ticket sales, which is important to be aware of. The transaction fee is a good place for merchants to lose track of the conversation and not actually take the time to calculate the average ticket of their sales and do the math. Of course there are other factors that affect every transaction. Several years ago, when the card brands went public and became responsible to pay returns to investors/stockholders, a new fee called Name Association and Brand Usage (NABU) appeared. They are currently less than two cents ($0.02) per transaction, but still adds to the overall costs for business owners, especially for merchants with LOW average tickets and HIGH transaction volumes. The rules are always being adjusted and changed as new laws are created by Congress and new regulations from FCC, FTC, and CFPB to name a few.

Along with other government legislation and regulation, the payments industry applies self-regulation to prevent over involvement from the government. Don't forget these companies must be profitable to continue to provide this valuable service. A question that you might want to stop and ask yourself is, "With the rules always changing, how do I play a game that I don't know the rules to?" Answer: You find a good coach or knowledgeable certified payments professional (CPP). Later we will provide a link to search for CPPs in your area. Next is an example of two merchants with the same rate and card volumes but, they have completely different processes and outcomes.

3.1 The Steakhouse and the Taco Stand

Let me explain the importance of average sale ticket and why the same rate plan doesn't necessarily equate to the same or equal costs. Here is an example that explains average ticket size and the effect that a transaction fee has when it converted into a rate.

Example:

Two restaurants both processed the same card volumes at the SAME RATES and SAME TRANSACTION FEES; their costs should be the same, right? It may sound correct but the total fees or cost will wind up being completely different. How is that possible you ask? Let's look at the example below:

Restaurant A. (Taco Stand)

Restaurant B. (Steakhouse)

Rate 1.55% and $0.17 per transaction

Rate 1.55% and $0.17 per transaction

Amount Processed $100,000

Amount Processed $100,000

Restaurant A's merchant fees: $3200.00

Restaurant B's merchant fees: $1720.00

This is of course, only an example of rate differences. However, I seek to illustrate the point that RATE is used as a distraction and without considering other factors is meaningless.

In this example Restaurant A is Bob's Taco Stand and Restaurant B is Bob's Prime Steakhouse. The taco stand has a much lower ticket than the steakhouse and therefore the steakhouse has far fewer transactions. You see $0.17 is 1.70% of a $10.00 sale but only 0.17% of a $100.00 sale. So on a low ticket sale the transaction fee is more of the cost than the rate. On the contrary, the higher the ticket on the sale the more important the rate becomes. Because of this, the transaction fee cost becomes less of the cost of the transaction or less significant.

Transaction Fee $0.17 / $10.00 =1.70%

Transaction Fee $0.17 / $100.00 = 0.17%

My point here is only an example and only touches the surface of how merchants are charged for processing. If you find this example to be a bit confusing that is because it is supposed to be. Certified Payment Professionals are there to assist you in navigating your way out of the rough waters of payments processing and get you to smooth sailing in those rough waters.

4.0 Two Types Of Merchant Accounts

Remember that choices are key when it comes to selecting the proper merchant services plan for your business model and the future of that business. Your goal should be to match your business up with the proper product to allow your business to grow and expand. Before we discuss that, we need to note that currently there are basically two different types of merchant accounts. These include Aggregate Risk and Traditional Risk models. Many of the mobile phone apps that you see out there that allow people to accept cards on their cell phones with little or NO monthly fees are Aggregate Risk accounts. This means that your transactions are lumped in with other merchants or users and the risk of the portfolio is shared. With a Traditional Risk Merchant Account the business or merchant is viewed as an individual and the risk is not shared, instead it is based on your business only and not others as well. Which one is right for you? I once heard an insult that rang a bit true to me, and so it stuck. If your business is making less than $5000.00 a month you have a hobby, not a business. It is a harsh statement to make, but there is some truth to that number.

I understand small beginnings, in fact I cherish them. Google, Microsoft, and Apple all started out in a garage somewhere so if you are a very small business please do not take offense. In fact, my first book, Auto Pilot Income, was written with startups in mind. Working from home and owning your own business is a great gig, but what happens when it really takes off? If you start a small business and do not plan to grow larger than $5,000 per month in credit card sales, you may be a good candidate for an aggregate model, like this one that we offer,

WWW.ALLPAYUSA.COM.

In fact, you can sign up today as an individual if you just want to be able to accept cards from friends or roommates. You can also sign up as a business if you have a business and you want to start accepting electronic payments from customers. Here is the math on why the $5,000 in card volume is the tipping point. Some Aggregate SAAS products have NO monthly fees, while Traditional Merchant Accounts do. Aggregate Models do not have PCI DSS and IRS TIN regulations and fees. You might be saying to yourself right now, "You lost me, what?" Okay, PCI or PCI DSS.

Payment Card Industry Data Security Standards Self Assessment Questionnaire must be completed by every merchant who processes cards. It must be completed annually or the Merchant Account will be fined for noncompliance. The fines usually range from $20 to $50 per month until the Questionnaire is completed. Back on topic, PCI fees, just to be enrolled are usually between $5 and $15 per month without any fines. That enrollment fee along with the IRS TIN Validation Fee of $5 per month means that a Traditional Merchant Account has fixed expenses of approximately $20 per month. If you are only processing say $2,000 per month that $20.00 is 1% without ever even running a transaction. Now, many of you are saying to yourself, "Wow, this guy has given this way too much thought." But that is exactly what merchants need to consider doing or if not, retain a trusted professional who will. To recap, small startups that plan on remaining small should consider some of our Aggregate Model Partners. For merchants and businesses looking to be scalable there are many products and companies that can achieve those goals very well too. The best thing to do is to get a CPP that you trust and have them head up your project.

4.1 Pricing Models

Pricing models include Tiered, Cost Plus, ERR/ Enhanced Rate Reduction, Flat Rate, Cash Discount or Surcharging, and Membership Plans. For years the interchange was simplified and only needed a few levels including Retail/Face to Face and MO/TO or Mail Order Telephone Order. These were just two basic ways to pay because everything was CREDIT CARDS as the Debit Card/Check Card had not been invented yet. However, with the introduction of new business models like Internet/e Commerce and the introduction of new card products known as Debit Cards, Reward Cards, Travel and Entertainment Cards, and Corporate Cards, new levels of Risk had to be attached to each type of sale, sale amount, and business risk factor. We can go much deeper here and explain that each business model falls under a MCC merchant category code or a SIC standard industry code as one element of the formula. Other elements are average ticket and the way the electronic data is being read or entered. Data entry methods such as Swiped, Keyed, and Chip Read may all be factors that affect the cost of that transaction. The verification method, how the transaction is being validated, signature, PIN, Mobile Phone, or no verification at all, can all be factors of the final cost of that transaction.

Myth-Busting The Merchant Payments Industry

Tiered Pricing was the least complicated and most profitable pricing model for the acquiring banks and their partners. It basically dumped transactions into Low risk, Medium risk, and High risk categories. Merchant companies would tease merchants and express or advertise the lowest rates and then quietly mention, or never mention, the Medium and High Risk categories. They would also fail to explain how and why a transaction can fall into those rate categories. Later, when the associations went to being publicly traded they publicized the Interchange Reimbursement Fees and many Merchant Companies started pricing merchants more straightforward with I/C Plus or Interchange Plus. That is a method of passing ALL of the costs to the merchant and then adding a fee of Basis Points and Pennies to each transaction as a commission to the merchant acquiring company. This is the most transparent plan out there, but there are still tactics that unethical agents use to confuse or misguide merchants. Some don't even know they are doing that, it just happens to be the way that they were trained. This is one of the unfortunate aspects of the industry.

ERR, Enhanced Rate Reduction, is a plan that is designed to look like a low rate but has a bump that raises rates and disqualifies certain transactions. I like to call it "smoke and mirrors". Flat Rate is just that. Flat Rate with some strings attached such as monthly minimums and membership fees can equate to rates being much higher when you add the fees and look at the math like we will shortly. CAsh Discount is a method where a sign is placed in the store that all of the prices are marked as a cash sale prices. When a card is presented the terminal will calculate a fee and add that fee to the customer's receipt as a separate line item that will say convenience or service fee. Last is a new method known as Membership programs. This is usually I/C Plus One monthly fee based on your volume and an additional penny cost per transaction which depends on the monthly fee. The higher the monthly fee, the lower the penny cost. The lower the monthly fee, the higher the penny cost. All of these programs can be fair to the merchant, but it is usually time consuming for many small business owners. If taken the time to understand the industry, who could we trust? That is why I wrote this book. Many merchants want to know if I can abbreviate the entire process, can I boil it all down to one number? Yes, which brings us to the question which is the title of the next short chapter.

4.2 Rate Vs. Cost

"What is your rate?" This is the most common question that a merchant asks a payments sales agents and it is a bad one.

Rate is only a small part of the equation. This is like asking a car dealer, "What is the gas mileage on this vehicle?" without any regard for the sticker price or payment and then making the decision to purchase based on gas mileage information only. It sounds foolish, doesn't it? Or Asking a pizza shop, "how much is a pizza?" we know they will need to know other factors like size, and toppings, before they can answer the question with some degree of accuracy. The same applies with payments. How do you know the proper question to ask to get you the right information that you need to make a good decision to fit your business model and product pricing? Don't worry, I will answer that question next.

4.3 Effective Rate: The Keys to the Ferrari

We have learned that the Rate is not Cost, and that there are other variables that need to be summed up to get to the truth. Now you will learn what effective rate is and what two numbers you need to use to make the calculation.

What is effective rate and why is it so important for merchants to know? Use this formula and use it every single month. Effective Rate, or Overall Rate, is the bottom line overall cost for a merchant to process cards. No one can tell you your future effective rate, it can only be calculated after the sales have been ran, totals have been tallied, and the charges have been published. Here is how simple the formula is to compute yourself each month. Take your TOTAL CARD FEES AND DIVIDE BY THE TOTAL CARD SALES VOLUME. For example, if your Total Merchant Processing Bill for your small business is $297.00 and your Total Card Volume is $10,000, then your Overall Effective Rate is 2.97%.

The lesson to be learned here is not to ask, "What is my rate?", but rather to ask, "Given my average ticket and business model, what do you expect my effective rate to be?" If the merchant sales representative answers you honestly they will not be able to give you a number. The reason is that we don't know how many cards we will take, and even more important to mention is that we have no way of knowing what types of cards may come through the door. I look at merchants and say, "Unless you have a crystal ball, no one can answer that question." What some merchants might consider doing is deciding up front during your business model planning phase what effective rate is acceptable to your business model and ask your representative to keep you under that rate or allow you to look for service elsewhere without penalty of cancellation.

5.0 Why The Merchant Services Industry Is Broken

Unlike many industries, a merchant service industries agent is not required to pass a test or even receive one hour of training before soliciting a merchant for their merchant account. This to me is the most troubling and unfortunate circumstance and the reason that the industry is hated by so many. The banks had an enormous business expense in processing paper checks and therefore banks had a great incentive to create a behavior pattern for customers to switch and use debit cards instead. The icing on the cake was that this method not only saved them money, but actually made them money. The need for banks to hire marketing arms to sell card services to merchants increased dramatically as Debit Card usage boomed. Those marketing arms, or ISO's / Independent Sales Organizations, in order to grow fast, did and still do mass hiring of anyone willing to try. These hired hands and fingers are far away from the brain, the actual product, or company that they represent. In many cases "agents" don't know the names and players of the companies processing the actual transactions. These salespeople, in their defense, are selling products that are constantly changing and frequently being reinvented and rebranded. This makes training difficult because it is too costly and time consuming, and thus defeats the purpose of the goal of gaining more and more merchant acceptance accounts. Here's an example of this. Bob owns a small market and his friend, Joe, is hired by a company with a fancy "bank like" name, First XYZ Merchant's Processing Company. Joe tells Bob how he is going to increase his business and help it grow. Bob jumps on board and signs a thirty page contract without reading it or having Joe explain it to him. Joe just started last week and doesn't really know anything other than the fact that he will be paid a few hundred dollars to have Bob sign that paper. Once he does, Bob is turned over to customer support in some other state and Joe is moving on to his next victim or in many cases, quits, which is even worse because now the merchant has no point of contact and is left to deal with the processor without agent assistance. This is unfortunately a typical scenario for many merchants until another fast talker promises more than Joe, and the problem repeats itself over and over until someone with knowledge and ethics arrives to actually help the merchant gain the help that they truly need. To recap, the industry grew too fast and the players were not required to train or certify the sales agents. It was a disaster waiting to happen. The Electronic Transactions Association is the premier trade association for the Financial Technical Payments industry. Software, hardware companies, financial institutions, and security companies all join the ETA to exchange information, network, and attend conferences to make the payments industry better as a whole for everyone. The ETA began a certification program called Certified Payments Professional. We will talk more about CPP's and how to find the right one, but first, below is a list of things to ask anyone soliciting you for service. My job here is to give you the training to get tough in this area and arm you with the tools to hit back.

5.1 Know Your Rights and Ask Good Questions

Are you a Certified Payments Professional listed on the Electronic Transactions Associations registry? If they are not, move on and find a Certified Payments Professional you can trust working with the public.

What other businesses like mine do you have locally? Ask for references and CALL THEM.

What is your customer service number and hours of operation? Place a test call.

Will you be my local agent?

What will it cost me to run a transaction the way I run transactions and based on my average ticket?

How do you secure the transactions?

Who is the acquiring bank?

Do you have a list of reasonably priced hardware?

Will I be provided the "Program Guide"? This is the 30 to 35 pages of fine print that should come with every merchant account but many times does not.

Do you offer ZERO CANCELLATION FEES? Will you earn my business each month and if not am I free to find another service without penalty?

5.2 Making Your Best Choice

There are so many companies and banks to choose from, who is the best choice for your business? This is not an easy question. The first thing that usually happens is that you go to your bank to open your business checking account and they ask, "Would you like to accept payment cards?" You answer, "Yes, of course" and they sign you into a 3 year contract with a processor that they work for. There are several problems here. First, these contracts almost always have cancellation fees to exit and sometimes they are renewable and very difficult to exit. Second, most banks DO NOT process payments, processing companies do. Currently, there are only two major banks who happen to own a processing company, but even they are separate entities with a different name than the bank who owns them. What this all means is that if you process through a big bank you are possibly unknowingly using a middleman. This middleman has huge overhead like branch offices, employees with benefits and pensions, pay to retired employees, and not to mention stockholders to answer to. Third, that person at your bank signing you up is most likely not your agent and will not likely be able to assist you with installation and service for your account because they are only a conduit for the bank and the processor. Of course, there are some exceptions to this but for the most part, this is how it is done. Remember that 90% of the transactions are processed by the top 5 processors. So, how should you go about getting the best agent and assistance for the entire time that you process payments? Find an Electronic Transactions Association Certified Payments Professional. When searching for a CPP try to find an independent agent that works with the public. Many CPP's work for the bank or financial institution and do not work directly with the public. You should be looking for someone who has multiple relationships with multiple processors, hardware, and software solution providers. Let's face it, choices are important when it comes to your business model and payments processing. Would you go to an ice cream stand with one flavor or thirty one flavors? It's nice to have choices. A CPP, what is a CPP? It is a new designation given by the ETA or Electronic Transactions Association. It is awarded, or earned by individuals who have at least three years of payments industry experience. To be recommended by other payments companies they must pass a rigorous examination, swear to pure ethics, and continue education credentials every three years or they will lose their status. This helps to ensure that you have a vetted, knowledgeable, and professional to assist you. Remember, find a CPP that works with the public and that works for you.

Glossary of Industry Terms as of 2017

Merchant Services Glossary

ABA Routing Number

Also referred to as a Transit Routing Number. Directs electronic ACH deposits to the proper bank institution.

ACH (Automated Clearing House)

The paperless funds transfer system maintained by the Federal Reserve or other entities that have networks to exchange electronic funds transfer items.

Acquirer

Any bank, financial institution, and public or private company that maintains a seller's credit card processing relationship and receives all transactions from the seller to be distributed to the credit card issuing banks.

Address Verification Service (AVS)

A service provided in which the seller verifies the cardholder's address with the issuing bank. Address verification does not guarantee that a transaction is valid.

Adjustment

A debit or credit to a cardholder or seller account to correct a transaction error.

Arbitration

The process followed by the Card Associations to determine whether an Issuer or an Acquirer has the ultimate responsibility for a chargeback. Either member initiates this process after the representment process is completed.

Authorization

Approval of a bankcard transaction by the card-issuing banks or approved independent service providers for a specified dollar amount. An authorization only indicates the availability of the card member's credit limit at the time the authorization is requested.

Authorization Response

The reply to a request for approval on a transaction.

Authorization Response Code

A code returned in the authorization response to indicate approval of a transaction. The code is recorded on the transition receipt as proof of authorization.

Back-end Processor

A data processing company that contracts with acquirers to provide communication and processing systems that connect with the interchange systems for clearing and settlement services on behalf of those acquirers. (In some cases the acquirer may act as its own back-end processor.)

Bankcard

Any valid card issued by a payment network or other card issuing organization that is presented in payment for goods and services or to obtain cash advances.

BIN (Bank Identification Number)

The 6-digit range of numbers assigned by the Federal Bureau of Standards and used by card companies to identify their financial transactions. The Discover® range begins with '6' (6xxxxx), the Mastercard® range begins with '2' (2xxxxx) or '5' (5xxxxx), and the VISA® range begins with '4' (4xxxxx).

Card Not Present Transactions

Transactions that are processed without the card or the cardholder being present, e.g., phone or internet orders.

Card Present Transactions

Transactions in which the cardholder and the card are present.

Cardholder

A person or entity that is issued a credit or debit account that is accessed through the use of a card.

Chargeback

When a credit card transaction is disputed (either at the request of the cardholder or by a card issuer), the dispute is handled through a chargeback. A chargeback will cause the amount of the original sale and a chargeback fee to be deducted from the checking or savings account provided. A chargeback is when a merchant has been found at fault in the dispute and money is removed from the merchant's account and reapplied to the buyer's account as a refund.

Clearing

The transfer of data between issuers and acquirers.

Contactless Payments

Contactless payments are transactions that use chip based technology and require no physical connection between the payment device (a card or mobile device) and the physical merchant terminal.

Control Number

Number that uniquely identifies a retrieval request or a chargeback.

Credit/Pending Settlement

Transactions of this status have been entered as credits but have not yet been submitted for settlement. These transactions will remain in this unsettled state until they are submitted for settlement. Once a credit has been settled, its status changes to credited.

Credit Slip

A paper or electronic representation of credit that is issued to a Cardholder on a prior credit card sale.

CVV2/CVC2

CVV2/CVC2 is the three-digit value printed on the signature panel on the back of cards immediately following the card account number. The 3-digit value helps validate that the cardholder has a card in his or her possession and the card account is legitimate.

Discount Rate

A discount rate is a fee associated with collecting, assessing, approving, processing, and settling credit card transactions. This fee is often a percentage of the transaction value.

EMV

EMV stands for Europay, Mastercard and Visa. EMVCo sets the standards for EMV chip cards and EMV terminals. Many countries worldwide already use the EMV chip card technology.

EMV Chip Cards

EMV chip cards have an embedded microchip that stores customer data. The chip is much more difficult to counterfeit than a magnetic stripe because the information on the chip changes with each transaction.

Fees

Fees for screening and processing online payments may include, but are not limited to, costs for the following:

- Monthly Account
- Discount rate
- Per item charges for credit card and electronic check transactions

Imprint

When a credit card cannot be swiped through a terminal, it is necessary to obtain an emboss of the card by using a manual imprinter.

Interchange Fees

Fees generally collected from acquirers on the value of their card sales and paid to issuers.

Issuer

Any Discover®, Mastercard®, American Express or VISA® member, or a commercial organization that establishes and maintains customer credit lines that are accessed through the use of a card. (Public and private companies and financial institutions that offer card-accessed lines of credit to consumers and businesses.)

Magnetic Stripe Reading

The credit card is swiped through the terminal to record the card information. Obtaining a magnetic stripe reading proves the card's presence at the time of a transaction.

Mastercard®

A registered mark for Mastercard International, Inc.

MATCH

A shared database maintained by the payment networks that lists all sellers terminated for cause by acquirers.

MCC or MCC Codes

Special numbers assigned by the payment networks to Seller types for identification and tracking purposes. Mastercard® uses MCC (Merchant Category Code), while VISA® uses SIC (Standard Industry Codes).

NFC

Near Field Communication (NFC) technology enables devices in close proximity to communicate. Payment transactions using NFC technology require a contactless merchant terminal and an NFC-enabled mobile device.

Payment Gateway

An e-commerce application service that authorizes card payments.

Payment Network

Any entity formed to administer and promote credit cards, including but not limited to Mastercard International, VISA U.S.A., or VISA International, that are licensing and regulatory agencies for credit card activities.

Quasi-cash Purchase

A transaction representing sale of items that are directly convertible to cash such as money orders and traveler's checks.

Re-presentment

The resubmission by an acquirer of a previously charged back sale in an attempt to recharge the cardholder. Chargebacks require some form of additional documentation confirming the validity of the charge and disputing the chargeback reason.

Retrieval Request

A retrieval request occurs when your customer requests more information about a transaction that appears on his or her credit card statement.

Return Policy

The merchant's limitations and/or requirements on accepting returned merchandise.

Sales Draft

The paper or electronic evidence of a purchase.

Secure Payment Page

A secure payment page assures customers that their payment information is encrypted for privacy and data integrity before it's sent over the internet. This page is typically identified by the "s" in https:// (instead of http://). Payment gateway providers make this necessary e-commerce link possible by hosting the payment gateway software and individual secure payment pages on their own servers.

Seller or Online Seller

An individual or business that sells products or services and is capable of accepting payment for products and services via a seller account.

Seller Account or Online Seller Account

The bank account a seller identifies as the sole account from which monthly and/or transaction fees are debited.

Seller Bank

(Acquirer or Processor) The financial institution with which a seller contracts to accept credit cards for payment of goods and services.

Seller Fees or Fees

Sellers are charged several types of fees for screening and processing online payments. Fees for products and services include, but are not limited to, costs for the following:

- Monthly Online Seller Account

- Discount rate
- Per item charges for credit card and electronic check transactions
- Chargebacks

Settlement

The process of transferring funds for sales and credits between acquirers and issuers, including the final debiting of a cardholder's account and crediting a seller's account.

Shopping Cart

In online marketing, a piece of e-commerce software on a web server that allows visitors shopping at an internet site to select items for eventual purchase.

SIC or Standard Industry Codes

Special numbers assigned by the Card Associations to Seller types for identification and tracking purposes. Mastercard® uses MCC (Merchant Category Code), while VISA® uses SIC (Standard Industry Codes).

Transaction

An act between a seller and a cardholder that results in either a paper or an electronic representation of the cardholder's promise to pay for goods or services received from the act.

Unauthorized Transaction

Any sale for which a cardholder does not provide his or her specific authorization. (This should not be confused with the failure to receive an authorization response from the issuer.)

VAR

Value added reseller, or a third-party providing card payment processing products or services, such as gateway provider, third party software providers, gift and loyalty providers. Essentially any product or service that supports, or integrates with your merchant account.

Thank you for studying this material.

Please check out my other book:

<u>Auto Pilot Income</u>: **How to automatically make more time and money**

Information is available on my website:
www.AllCardUSA.net

"Finally the truth is explained and the Game is over for any business owner who takes the short time that I spent reading this book. I never knew what the truth was until now. This knowledge is a huge asset to my business. I wish I knew then what I know now. Thanks Bart !"   M. Blake

"Thank you for breaking things down in simple terms. It all seems so simple now."   C. Folk

"Anyone who tries to travel the rocky roads of business, with just the thought of cost in mind, without someone (like Bart) who actually knows where the potential pit falls are, deserves the inevitable loss of their merchant number and closing of business."   T. Bauer

Bart Kohler, CPP

Myth-Busting The Merchant Payments Industry
A Merchants Guide to the Truth and Higher Profits